How to survive
The cold
With a big nose.

Conor Nixon

NOSE EVERYTHING

Surviving the cold with a big nose.

Copyright © 2018 Conor Nixon

All rights reserved

ISBN-13:978-1-9999759-1-3

DEDICATION

Anyone who has gone through ridicule for having a larger nose than normal, this is for you. Big noses are beautiful. Peace out.

Surviving the cold with a big nose.

Surviving the cold with a big nose.

CONTENTS

- Acknowledgments 7
- Ancient nose sketch 8
- Nose's 9
- Body heat 10
- How to warm up your nose 11
- Keep your nose healthy 18
- A Runny nose 22
- Nose hairs 27
- Drinking hot liquids 29

(Bonus content)

- Insults you might encounter 31
- Activity 32

- About the author 33

Surviving the cold with a big nose.

ACKNOWLEDGMENTS

There are several people to thank for helping with this book. My wife Michelle who puts up with my nose, it can't be easy for her and for always being on hand when I can't think of the word I need. Ian Mc Sorley for being a great model and nose mentor. I guess I should thank my parents for my nose. It's weird that I am the only one of 5 children that came out with a big nose. Even my twin has a lovely sized nose. I just had a son of my own and I pray to God everyday he doesn't get my nose. So far so good.

Surviving the cold with a big nose.

Ancient nose sketch

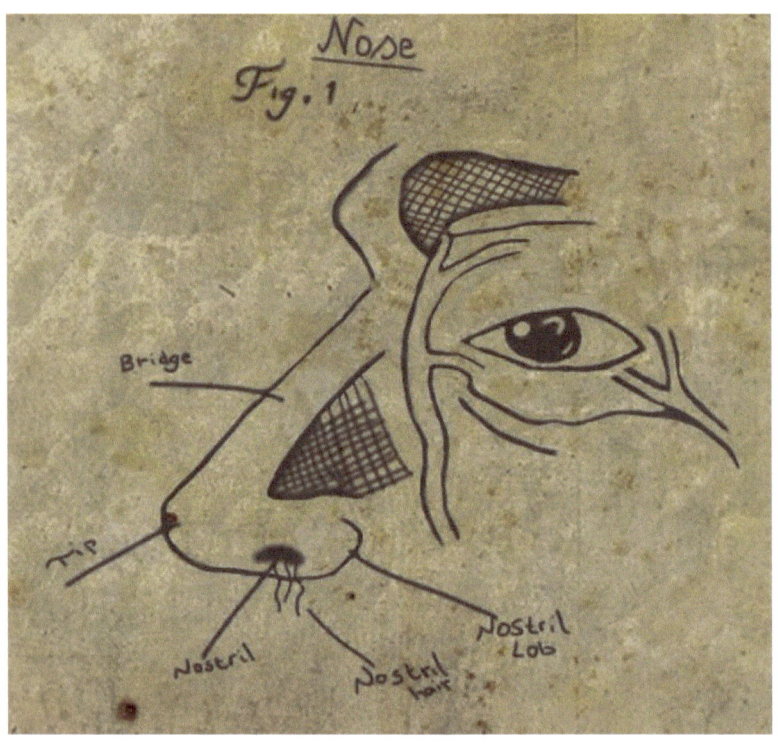

NOSES

Noses. We all have one. A compulsory piece of equipment used for smelling purposes, (and breathing), they come in all shapes and SIZES. If you are reading this, more than likely you have a big nose. Well do not worry and don't get upset as 1 in 4 humans have a big nose. (stat may have been fabricated)

Protecting yourself against the cold has become perfected in recent years with hats, scarves, gloves and jackets widely available. However, the nose can be forgotten about.

In this book you will learn vital knowledge of nose survival in cold and adverse environments. This important information has been passed down by our big nosed ancestors and I am about to share the secrets so you can use them and protect your nose for the rest of your life.

BODY HEAT

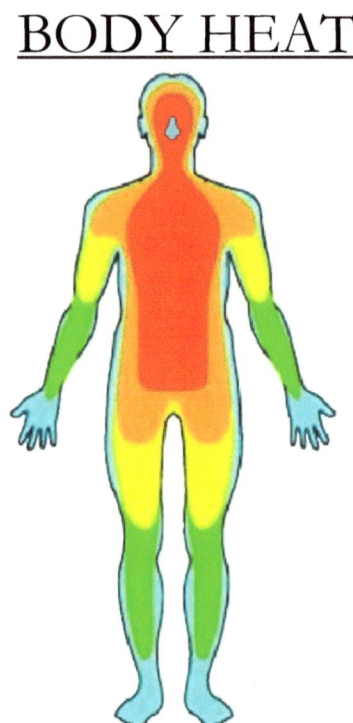

If you let your nose get too cold your body will automatically try and warm it up. This is perfectly normal, it is your bodies response to the cold. This isn't a problem with most, BUT, if you have a nose that is further away from your face, your body will draw heat away from your vital organs to warm it up. If this happens you can get nose frost bite (frost bite of the nose) or go into nose-thermia.

Thankfully it is 100% preventable.

HOW TO WARM UP YOUR NOSE

This is Ian. He will demonstrate the techniques for warming up your nose.

Surviving the cold with a big nose.

❖ Using your hands

- Cup your hands together.

- Put your hands around your nose and mouth like Ian shows you here.

- When you breath naturally into your hands your warm breath will heat your cold nose up nicely.

CAUTION When using this technique make sure you have fresh breath. The last thing you want is to be sniffing in stinky breath.

Surviving the cold with a big nose.

❖ <u>Using a lighter</u>

- Get a lighter.

- Ignite the lighter.

- Carefully bring the lighter towards your nose.

- Stop when you feel the heat from the flame.

> This method will quickly restore your nose to its optimum temperature.
>
> **CAUTION** Be careful you don't burn the beak of yourself or singe your nostril hair.

Surviving the cold with a big nose.

❖ Using a hot drink

- Get a cup of tea/coffee/hot chocolate etc.

- Hold it up to your nose.

- The steam from the liquid will warm the nose up in a jiffy.

CAUTION Do not look down when using this technique or you will burn the tip of your nose.

(more on this on page 31)

Surviving the cold with a big nose.

KEEP YOUR NOSE HEALTHY

Surviving the cold with a big nose.

One of the dangers of having a big nose is Nose chap. Basically its extreme chapping of the skin on the nose. You can prevent this from happening your large nose.

HOW?

By simply moisturising your nose every morning. This is very important in all types of weather. The sun can wear away at the skin on your nose as well as the wind and rain.

You need to add it into your morning routine. My morning routine is as follows, I get out of bed. Stumble into the bathroom. Pee into the direction of the toilet. (Nobody is perfect am I right?) Flush the toilet. Wash my hands. Moisturise NOSE and face. Brush teeth and so on.

It fits right in. The change it makes to my nose is so good. It's never dry, it's NEVER chapped and it's never sore.

Totally worth adding into your morning routine.

Surviving the cold with a big nose.

Me moisturising the nose one morning.

There are a lot of moisturisers out there that you can use. I will name a few that I have used in the past and the one I'm using now.

1. Nivea for men. - Well-known brand in skin care. Not too expensive but it comes in a small tube.

2. Bull dog- Not the most well-known brand but it is a brilliant little moisturiser. Again, like the Nivea it comes in a small tube and with beaks like ours they would waste out in a week.

3. Dove- This is the moisturiser I used for a long time. Lasts ages and great protection against the elements. I would highly recommend this moisturiser.

4. E-45- My winner hands down is the E-45 moisturiser. Ticks all the boxes. Protects, extra-large pump action container and not too expensive for what you get.

1

2

3

4
MY TOP PICK

Surviving the cold with a big nose.

A RUNNY NOSE

Last thing you want to do is use your sleeve as a tissue!

Surviving the cold with a big nose.

A great tip would be to ALWAYS carry a packet of tissues with you. This shouldn't be ignored. A runny nose can be embarrassing, and you really don't want to use your sleeve as a hanky. If your friends see the "slug trails" left by the liquid boogers you will be mocked and ridiculed, and rightly so.

A simple pack of tissues can stop this. If you feel it running down towards your mouth quickly pull out the pack, take out a tissue and blow your nose.
(Always discard your tissues in a civilized manner!)

A good tip is to blow and wipe your nose with a tissue before it runs down your face.

ATTACK IS THE BEST FORM OF DEFENCE.

Surviving the cold with a big nose.

Ian just after blowing his nose into a cheap tissue.

This isn't an area where you should buy cheap. There can't be enough said for getting quality tissues. People with small nose's can get away with buying cheap tissues.

Buy, good, tough (but soft) rigorous, up to the challenge tissues.

Remember, there is A LOT of moisture up in our facial appendages. (Nose)

Cheap tissues will not stand up to it. Just take a look at the picture on the adjacent page of poor Ian after blowing his nose into a cheap tissue.

Skimp on other things like tea bags, sugar or even toilet paper.

DON'T SKIMP ON TISSUES.

Surviving the cold with a big nose.

NOSE HAIRS

Society says that we should always keep our nose hairs trimmed or cut. But, this is the leading cause of Nose frost bite and nose-ithermia in people with big noses. I can't stress this enough. Do not succumb to this social pressure.

The science behind why we have nose hair, goes like this.

Nose hair traps air and warms it to heat up the body. Cutting or trimming the nose hair lets 80% more cold air into the nostrils and can significantly cool the brain causing brain freeze. It also raises the risk of Nose frost bite and nose-ithermia which is a horrible condition where it is painful to sniff, sneeze and wipe.

An alternative to cutting or trimming your nose hairs is to hide them instead.

Here are two ways.

Surviving the cold with a big nose.

- If you have a beard, you can brush the nose hairs down into the moustache hairs. No one will ever know.

- Get some hair gel. Put a small/large (depending on the number of nose hairs) amount on your finger and push them bad boys back up your nose. This will last all day.

Surviving the cold with a big nose.

DRINKING HOT LIQUIDS

No matter what job you have, consuming hot drinks is an everyday occurrence, that most take completely for granted. For us in the big nose community though, we need to be extremely careful while completing this task.

For me personally, ever since I got 2nd degree burns as a direct result of drinking coffee from a wide mug I have certain rituals that I need to stick by when drinking hot liquids.

- ☐ Small cups.- This is so my nose stays on the outside of the cup and not into the hot abyss.

- ❖ Cool down- Let it cool down a bit before drinking. This means, that if your nose does happen to touch the liquid it won't get burned.

When getting a take away cup with a lid it can get embarrassing. Those lids are not made with large noses in mind. When I drink from the lid my nose always squashes against the lid and it is very awkward, uncomfortable and degrading.

In this case I always go without the lid. Dangerous as it is I am always extra careful.

When drinking hot drinks on cold days always take advantage of the steam. It can save your life. (see page 18)

Caution- Do not get burned because you held it too close. Don't let any nose juice fall into the drink. That would be yucky.

Insults you might encounter

- Some beak on you.
- King of the beaks.
- Leave some oxygen for the rest of us.
- You can smoke in the shower with that thing.
- You look very aero dynamic.
- All joking aside though, your nose is huge.
- You can see your nose from space.
- Did you tell lots of lies when you were young?
- You can smell things before they happen.
- Don't sleep on you back or you'll scratch the ceiling.
- You nearly poked my eye out with that thing.

Surviving the cold with a big nose.

Activity

Join the dots.

Surviving the cold with a big nose.

ABOUT THE AUTHOR

Conor Nixon is an Irish author based in Dundalk. Conor is a nose enthusiast. Conor is also a survival specialist and has gained a lot of knowledge about the Nose and its importance in keeping the body regulated. A happy Nose is a happy life.

Please consider :

- Subscribing to Conor Nixon Survival on YouTube

- Following @Conor Nixon Survival on Facebook and Instagram

- Following @The Nose Page on Facebook and Instagram.

- Write a review on Amazon.

Thank you all.

Protecting your nose is protecting your life.

(This nose belongs to Ian McSorley)

www.ingramcontent.com/pod-product-compliance
Lightning Source LLC
Chambersburg PA
CBHW041756040426
42446CB00001B/55